Emma Torrao is a poet and this is their first book. While finishing culinary school, Emma decided to also pursue writing. They developed a love for and refined their poetry skills during high school. They pull from their experiences to share their journey through prose as they live through growing pains, relationships, and body image challenges. Emma now lives in a mountain town where they continue writing in the shade of the Rockies.

To anyone who decided to just go for it. Giver'er.

Emma Torrao

NOT MY LIFE'S STORY

AUSTIN MACAULEY PUBLISHERS™

LONDON • CAMBRIDGE • NEW YORK • SHARJAH

Ordering Information
Quantity sales: Special discounts are available on quantity purchases by corporations, associations, and others. For details, contact the publisher at the address below.

Publisher's Cataloging-in-Publication data
Torrao, Emma
Not My Life's Story

ISBN 9798889108061 (Paperback)
ISBN 9798889108078 (ePub e-book)

Library of Congress Control Number: 2023924220

www.austinmacauley.com/us

First Published 2024
Austin Macauley Publishers LLC
40 Wall Street, 33rd Floor, Suite 3302
New York, NY 10005
USA

mail-usa@austinmacauley.com
+1 (646) 5125767

Thank you to my family for supporting me when I decided to take a leap of faith; and thank you to Austin Macauley for giving me the chance to try.

(I suppose that I should write an introduction but that seems futile. I'll hold myself to a painstaking standard and be upset when I am unavoidably rejected but not surprised. I'm a poet, not a novelist. this is not my life's story.)

This is not my life's story.

This is a story,
told in prose

with quotes in phrases tapped down to the page

I burnt at the edges just to keep you. Fraying edges grasp to keep you searching for love that was never there.

So I closed the box by turning the page a new start new clothes new home new aesthetic new person.

Same Being.

I unpack all the things you didn't like to decorate my body. Draping silks to hang delicately on the curves of my soul. New curtains and chandeliers, covering the chipped paint with a new color.

I unpack myself to erase you.

this is my introduction

My Dandelions and Chrysanthemums had become Roses to please You. So, I'll tear out all the Weeds you left in me. Out with the New and in with the Old. There is beauty in what was, even though it was lost, it refuses to be forgotten. Even the depths of time cannot and will not tame me.

Time is a goddess who is relentless and unforgiving. She is dressed in a sharp suit with a crystal ball to match. She ensures that all meet their end.

There is a Witch who lives in the woods behind my house. She is wild and untamable and beautiful.

All the adults talk about Her as if She has some sort of disease. I wonder how they would talk if they knew about Her slew of nighttime visitors.

They talk and She knows. It's what She wants.

She is intimidating to them because She doesn't live by their rules. She has morals not meant for mortal men. She is sucking the marrow out of life, letting the fires burn until their embers burn out. She loves freely with reckless abandon yet fully aware of the consequences. She is kind without rules, holding on until the end but flying free.

– Carpe Diem

When I was 10, they said,
"Why haven't you lost the baby fat yet?"

When I was 11, they said,
"You should consider working out."
When I was 12, they said,

"You should stop eating so many carbs."

When I was 13, they said,
"You're not pretty like the other girls."

When I was 14, they asked,
"Why are you so self-conscious?"

Because when I was never enough, they sought to point out my flaws, tearing out my imperfections and shoving them back in my face.

Suddenly I was 17.

On the days when I'm sure,
you say I love you
But when I say I don't know
you seemingly can't.

the sun can't shine forever.

There was a time when all I wanted was to be a Lady

Now I can't stand the thought

Pretty dresses mean weighted crowns
Expectations I can't keep; Promises I can't hold

The scars of people-pleasing reside in my soul
Anger and resentment burn deep in my lungs
Screams trapped within the walls of my mind.

These emotions pent up I am not the pop bottle metaphor.

I am Pompei, my skin does not contain me; you cannot fathom my power.

You manipulated me to protect yourselves but you cannot stop a tsunami once it has begun.

I was raised on the gender binary; Now I am the opposite.
I flow between masculine and feminine,
When thoughts of others are no longer a concern freedom
comes naturally.

I used to live in secret.

I am the culmination of all the people I have known.

My Smile comes from childhood friends whose faces I can't
remember.

My Anger is the burden of others who could never address
their problems.

I taught myself to fight when others left.

My Strength comes from the women who raised me, what
protects my strength is the love in their hearts.

My Intellect comes from teachers' adoration for their jobs
wanting to pass on knowledge.

My Laugh is simultaneously my own and everyone else's.
It rings from their jokes.

My Spirit is an heirloom passed down from fighters.
Their fierceness builds me up.

I don't understand gender.
I am restricted by the confines of my biology.
I am, other.

When I answer surveys,
I select the empty box.
Or I lie.

Why do I insist on
holding
on?

"Suck on the marrow,
don't choke on the bone!"
– John Keating
(Dead Poets Society, 1989)

"My skin is a canvas. I'll paint it with art."
– Le Tatouage

"My body is a temple. I'll decorate it with jewels."
– Les Bijoux

"My spirit is a gift. I'll treat it with respect."
– La Vie

I used to give more chances than deserved I built too many bridges only for them to be burnt down I let myself become battered and bruised I forced myself to change I walked out of the mold I am my own person I rejected their ideas I made my own I promised myself I would build myself.

I had to start from the ground up.

I felt the sun blister my skin and realized I was alive.

She sings anywhere and everywhere for everyone. Her honey voice pulls me to sleep.

If I could dream, they would be of her.

My love, the apple of my eye, the calm in my storm.

She doesn't need to change, she is good. What we've built together, what we will build. We talk of cats and trees and wall art and afternoon teas. Although we have separate dreams, we hope together.

–Nos rêves ensemble

When I am on my own, the world burns. I burn. Although I grow, my roots are singed, my branches are empty of leaves now turned to smoke and ash food for the fire that ravaged my spirit, scarred my bones.

I rebuilt myself into this body.

If you've a fire while the wood is still wet I applaud you I applaud the patience you possess of which I desire but hearths aren't candelabras.

My heart is a different shape than before.

My expensive candles made of beeswax and soy with wooden wicks in darling containers. They bring me a simple joy. Scented with aloe and smoke and lavender laces with vanilla leaving me content.

I'm all bent out of shape.

If you keep allowing a candle to burn before the layer is completely melted you get a ring of untouched wax It becomes the bane of your existence, ruining your candle. The ring will soon become a well.

melted candle wax burns.

The epitome of romance is hand written letters.

I'll pour my heart out to you.
Thoughts held together in a thick envelope and sealed with
wax.

I will wear my heart on my fingertips for you.

Your love is my religion.

I keep a tin of Quality Street candy on my desk. It doesn't contain any candy, only letters and cards, a few cool rocks, and the only medal I've ever won. I'll never show anyone the tin but one day, after I'm gone, maybe my family will find it and keep it; as a reminder of who I was, as I am now. Maybe this notebook will join it. The physical embodiment of my thoughts.

I always say I don't follow any religion but maybe I do. Maybe it's Writing. There are rules but there are also loopholes. I can pick and choose. My style is my own but others may call it freeform, say it's fantastical. But if Writing is my religion then Poetry and Dreams and Love and Creation and Spirit are my gods.

I put my soul into everything I do. My food and my writing contain carefully carved pieces of my spirit designed to fit like a glove, the next piece of the puzzle. These are the things I live for.

I've built my life around these things. Following Dreams. Loving Fiercely. Create Endlessly. Writing Poetry. Enduring Spirit. This is what I am. This is the shape of my soul.

Cookie cutters make sure that every cookie is the exact same but sometimes,

Heads get squished,

Petals spread a bit too much.

Corners get cut off.
So we cover them with icing, with chocolate.
But even then, mistakes can appear.

So we turn them into something where mistakes don't matter.
They have many, many names but I call them rum balls.
They're made from over-mixed cakes, over-baked cookies, and leftover pastry. Then we mix it together with chocolate and rum et voila. Even our mistakes can be useful.

Most often they are lessons learned through consequences but helpful all the same.

When I was in first grade, they told us bullying was bad.
That it was wrong.

But they turned a blind eye as other kids slaughtered my spirit.

A classmate's mother made me the villain, exploiting her position of power over a child.

Now my childhood is a blur, memories I no longer remember.

– La perte d'enfance

When I was four, I learned to read. Then I learned to write.

But first, I had to learn to talk.

The shapes were funny on my lips, crumbling on my tongue.

I was younger then.

Now I can do all three. In two languages. And yet I am still not smart enough.

There is a monster under my bed. It lives in a drawer, tucked in There used to be a gaping hole, a box. Sometimes, late at night, the monster escapes and resides in the lonely fissures of my consciousness,

The dreams are always the same.

I've been living with the monster so long that it no longer scares me.

Until the day that it moved to my chest.

There used to be a gaping hole,

now there is only a monster.

This monster does not have a name, it hardly even has a shape.

The hole itself is lumpy and misshapen, reminiscent of an anatomically correct heart with all its chambers and arteries.

The color is a deep, dark purple accented with bright blues. It's strange; how can something so terrible can look so lovely.

Anytime people ask about the monster, something Staples my mouth shut. It's too painful to pry the cold metal from my bloody skin.

I haven't decided which is worse.

I am trying to understand it.

If I can understand it, maybe I can get rid of it.

I wake every day to the sound of my alarm. The monster is curled up at my feet or by my back.

But I cannot move until it has returned to the hole in my chest.

Feeling empty or numb or angry I no longer have control.

I've been trying to replace the monster with something.

Some days, it's all I can do just to take shallow breaths. It leaves me feeling empty

People are exhausting. I appreciate that people all have unique needs but sometimes I have to prioritize my own.

Ambivert: one whose personality type is intermediate between extrovert and introvert.

– Dictionary.com

I can easily interact with others; I'm loud, excitable. I enjoy long conversations. But I have to be alone sometimes. It confuses most people.

There's a great big hole in my stomach. I'm trying to fill the
empty in my chest but no one is around. The storm came
during the night; aftershocks have gusted through the
atmosphere since the rains passed. I should be asleep; I
know they'll tell me that. I don't want to worry them. Now
I listen to sad music and hold my purple pen and purple
notebook. I want to stop thinking but it's too much work. I
need sleep but I don't want it. It burns the back of my mind.
I've been having strange dreams of late that leave me
feeling angry and cold and confused. I put up postcards on
the blank yellow walls of my room but it still feels empty.
I'm in a small town of less than 7,000 and the hurricane
leaves it feeling post-apocalyptic. I'm left alone with my
wandering mind trying to numb it with senseless media and
someone else's pain.

– 5,948 km away

I'm floating in the ravine as the current swirls around me. It
builds and crescendos and falls too fast.
I don't know what the raft is made out of and sometimes I
forget that it's there.

The rain is soft and gentle on my face.
Water droplets on the roof and windows.

I feel like as if I were a fraud, speaking of love, romance and affection as if I have ever received any.

I've tried to fathom an excuse, a reason as to why I am unlovable.

Is my stomach too soft?
My face too warm?
My thighs too wide?
Do I carry too much weight on my shoulders, too much history in my bones?

Am I too loud to be held?
Do my lips taste a little too familiar?
When I sing, do you hear someone else?

I'm so tired and it's not the kind that you can simply sleep
Away.

The exhaustion fills my bones replacing the marrow, it floods the chambers of my heart, overtaking my blood.

I am impossibly hungry with nothing to satiate my needs.
I've locked myself away and smashed the key. If only I had
glue.

The growl of my empty stomach pulls me forwards i chase
another high.

You'd think that feeling forever watched would keep me
from feeling lonely.

I suppose that I should thank all the people who've seen me through to this point of my life. Whether they stayed or not. this is the first time I've truly shared my art. wanted to share my art. poetry is deeply personal; it's all the thoughts I've decided should be just for me. even though people I know have similar thoughts and share them aloud. feelings are not dirty: they are not wrong. they can be extreme, messy or confusing even. writing is my therapy. I tried to be a novelist, someone who writes short stories. I've never completed a novel and only finished drafts of a handful of short stories. my sister is a playwright, a wordsmith, a painter with words. yet her works are never over flowery. I like flowers; their powerful perfumes and vibrant colors drown my senses. it's childish. I was never truly allowed to be a child as the eldest daughter of three. two daughters and a son. for all their mistakes my parents loved me. it's perfectly evident in pictures, their voices as they ask me about my college education.

Apparently, eldest children are the most likely to attend a post-secondary institution of some kind. I don't know if this is true.

I'm rambling now. It's out of my hands now.

– I'm trusting you now.

People are often confused by Hephasetus and Aphrodite.
They are two people defined by their bodies.
One, too beautiful to be real.
The other, too hideous to bear looking.

In reality, it makes perfect sense.
Love is looking deeper, going past surface flaws.

The legend of Hephaestus and Aphrodite is framed as such:
A forced marriage,
A torrid affair,
A lonesome and empty relationship.

In truth, the pair worshiped each other; peering past facades
and superficial traits.

As children, we are taught that the only fulfilling
relationships we can have are romantic and sexual.

To completely disregard the depths of affection a person can
feel,
it's a crime.

The Greeks have seven words for Love,
each a God in their own right,
the Children of Aphrodite.
Eros, Lust-filled passion.

Philia, Affectionate and friendly.
Storge, Unconditional, familial.
Agape, Selfless and for all.
Ludis, Playful and flirtatious.
Pragma, Committed and long lasting.
Philautia, Love for oneself.
As young women, we are confined to our bodies
but not allowed to care for them.
We are never good enough.

Aphrodite is considered to be the eldest of the Greek Gods,
the first to appear in their mythology.
Her powers keep the world turning yet,
She is reduced to looks.

But I refuse to be boxed in.

I'll walk a million miles,
map out all the stars,
plant all the flowers.
Simply to gain your affection.

As young girls, we are taught to confuse love with pain. If
a boy makes fun of you, he thinks you're pretty. Then we
are reprimanded for falling into toxic relationships, but if a
boy pushes you, he likes you.

Love is so immense,
Venus is the only Goddess to have a planet named after her!

Lovely Aphrodite,
when the Greeks began naming their gods,
it was she they first chose to personify.
Love, Lust, Beauty, Pleasure, and Passion.

– Lovely Aphrodite

Someone once wrote; you say you love the rain, but you open your umbrella. You say you love the sun, but you find a shadow spot. You say you love the wind, but you close your windows. This is why I am afraid when you say you love me too.

I am not afraid.

Actually, that's a lie.
I am absolutely fucking terrified.
But it's never for the reason that you think.

I'm so worried that I'm too young;
too young to know what I want,
differentiate between right and wrong,
too young to build something for myself, make something of myself,
too young to know just how much I love you.

It's been seared into my mind, branded on my skin
that I'm too young to be in love, yet
love is all I've ever known.

Guess I'm lucky in that regard.

When all my friends and classmates were watching their parent's divorces from afar,
I was watching them,
As they shattered, destined to repeat the mistakes of their parents.

I'm terrified of being alone.
I live on my own, take care of myself
I'm independent but I don't want to be lonely.

I read and write as a form of escapism.
I'm addicted to music.
It drowns out the background noise.

I talk the way I speak.
Well, sort of.

I should like to portray the aura of considerable erudition.
Polysyllabic, intelligent vocabulary.
I wholly understand what they mean.

Humans are like houses.
With a door and windows.
But you don't truly know them till
you are invited inside.

Come in, come in! they say in haste.
Now it's time for your tour of their world to begin.

We start in your entry
With the shoes and jackets.
Hats and keys.
The first glimpse of your true nature.
Who are you?
What are you like?

Do you own military grade boots or
Rupaul runway worthy stilettos?
Jackets for usefulness or
Jackets for fashion?
Your keys, what are they for?
Your house, car or
are they for something else?

We go into the living room.
Filled with pictures, books, films, art, and memorabilia.
Do you like history or science fiction?
Monet or Picasso?
Green Day or Imagine Dragons?
Montgomery or Verne?

The pictures living on the mantel tell
A story.
Your family.
However big or small.
Your friends.
Precious memories.
Even the paint on the wall
hears and sees.

Even the kitchen can tell you stories.
The fridge filled with your favourite foods.
The dishes hold secrets from dinner parties and birthdays.
The chairs contain the words of the people who sat there.
The floor holds the sounds of the lonely nights.

The bathroom.
Is it filled with self care products or
is it empty?
Is the medicine cabinet full?
How do you care for yourself?

The basement, filled with memories you don't tend to share.
Only the closest see.
The pain.

The joy.
Secrets only the close tend to share.

Finally, the bedroom.
The room that holds your heart.
The keeper of the deepest, darkest secrets.
What it hides,
stays untold.
How do you identify yourself?

Humans are like houses.
Our bones the structure that supports our minds.

When we are born, the houses are empty.
Only filled with the basic furnishings.
As we age,
the houses age.
When we die, the aged houses remain with our memories.

– Humans Are Like Houses

Love, isn't it beautiful?
Unique in all its beautiful glory.

Wouldn't it just be perfect if we could
run away into our own little
imaginary dream world?

Our love is spilled across ceramic tiles,
like butter and honey on toast.
A deliciously kept secret,
Just for the two of us.

Keep it sacred,
lost under fresh linen.
It burns bright at the end of the tunnel.
We are magic.
Creating peace at the Eye of the

Storms move swiftly, breaking things.
trust is a casualty
Luck bruised by hate
bringing only pain.

Lost in the dark,
no light to guide us
moving forward towards an empty pit.

The answer is right there,
Shining blood spilled across white, ceramic tiles.

– Our Tragic Love Story

she smells like fresh linen like parchment her skin is soft like silk and smooth like cream her eyes hide pools of galaxies her pigment is bright as fresh coffee it glows like gold in the sun her lips drenched in shimmering liquid taste of sugar and rum the light of her soul sets the world on fire she is pure diamond with rough, sharp edges that cut like a knife yet she is soft you can't survive her depth but she is all you crave no one can compare.

no one flinches when she undresses as her hands cradle sweet nothings float past her strawberry mouth the rain lands on her like dreams to a pillow her clothes drenched to the bone her hair is matte yet ever more beautiful her laughter is a song that never ends more contagious than before there are none so graceful, so serene she fills holes you never knew where there.

the world could end tomorrow and I would spend it getting lost in her eyes counting the freckles on her cheeks because they are precious jewels our fingers intertwined legs tangled beneath the sheets it's too late to be awake but the taste of the conversation the candy that is her voice too sweet to sacrifice.

the kinks in her hair make me weak in the knees she flows like water and falls like the sun her beauty is not one of jealousy but one of passion the scars on her hands form hearts made of guitar strings caressing fingertips leave permanent marks on my thighs.

her body carved from marble coloured chocolate tinted with lavender billows like leaves time flies like wind when she smiles blooming flowers cry honey she lives so fiercely the ground trembles and the clouds burst at their seams she tames madness courts chaos breathes fire the curves of her form hold histories skin bleeds crimson stains like paint thick like blood.

broken when she sings love when she flies the earth turns night into day peacefully drains the well a ticking time bomb we get one life each day she thrives on joy a savior for the lost in the sky only falling into her embrace.

she remains free while promised to me the ring on a chain rest between her collarbones kissed skin stained red from lipstick roses wilting in the vase shrouded in shadows loose tears scattered across the pages breaking loose cannons a figment of my imagination she is loving without rules say not today we cling to when tomorrow belongs solely to her.

– Her

I Remember when the days were long and the
grass was green
The sky a kind blue reflected in our eyes.
The smiles small children wore showing
epiphanies of our happiness.
We were part of a world where everyone could be
merry.

I Remember the night we met under the bright
star light
Your smile outshone every hot ball of air the
space had gifted us
The air warm with the laughter of many
your eye's green like fresh leaves
In the early spring time.

I Remember when you said you loved me,
letting me know you wouldn't
let go.

I Remember when we ran away to the tree house.
Covered in miniature daisies,
gardenias,
lilies,
orchids,
and roses.

I Remember when I promised myself to you,
The ring never leaves our fingers.
I Remember You.

I'm here to apologize for all the pain that was caused
I can only assume that you had plans for us.
But that all went wrong.
It's just human nature to strive for perfection.

Or maybe it wasn't.
Maybe we made ourselves into this
Competing for who has more money,
more oil,
more land,
more weapons.

So you gave us family to teach us love
and we thought that meant a man and women and their
children.
So this is what it means: a basic social unit consisting of
parents and their children, considered as a group, whether
dwelling together or not:
But a family does not start when a child is born.

Family starts when people care for each other.
2 friends living together is family.
An old woman and her cats is family.
Family has no constraint,
no rules.

Except for one;
don't hurt the family.
And that's what we did.

The world is a family and humans are siblings.
But sons and daughters alike are enslaved,
totured,
Killed.

Mother Earth gave us the gift of life,
the ability to create life and we don't deserve it.

Humans can do so much good
but many of the ones in power wreak destruction.
But it keeps us in control.

I never know where I will go
It gets me every time.

I can plan as many routes as I want but,
My heart takes control.

I guess that is a problem.

I let emotion cloud my judgment.

I wonder,
Do others see me as weak because

I wear my heart on my
Sleeve?
Do I see myself that way?
Whenever I am alone my emotions take control.
My mind is lost to the wonder and awe and creativity
But,

It is also lost to pain.
And then I run.

To bed, to books, to art to blame.
I tell myself to stay put.

You can't run forever.
Maybe I can't run forever but
I sure can try.
I can never escape my mind.
Even as my feet pound on the
Pavement
I am lost to my own insanity.
But a smiling face
a welcome friend ends it all.
You can't run forever but you can recover.
When the flood comes crashing in,
there won't be fear, no noise just silence
filled with white noise crashing waves

Blooming seafoam colored teal tinted Red.

When the sky comes falling down,
do the stars stop working? Does love keep turning?
There is just a void, empty and unfeeling.
Was it worth it? Did I do enough?
How can the world continue moving as smaller ones
burn off cliff edges

Making points and breaking points determine our worth
decided by others pleased by our successes.

Drifting demons make deals, spin coins
Lawless angles collect souls enforcing right and wrong
Hypocritically.

State your name, entrance granted.
Lose it all on some wish.
Burning hell beats living a lie.

Stained black mold rotten mildew tar
it's all just luck off the draw.

this is a love letter.

this is a love letter to the one who has won my heart; a vagabond boy with ocean eyes roaming the cosmos in search of something.

whenever someone asks me why i love you, i simply smile and look away because if i gave them even one reason, everyone would fall in love with you.

i love everything about, you i endlessly adore you. i eternally crave your brilliantly beautiful smile. your blue eyes glimmer under the sun reflecting all the wonder that is you.

i love the way you make me smile, the curve of your lips pressed firmly against mine. the slight hook of your nose adds dimension to your face in a new and unprecedented way.

the square shape of your figure is relaxed by the slight curves of your hips. Your hands are soft, the lines running through them create a piece of art.

someone once asked me if i knew how much you loved me and said "yes, as many stars as there are in all of space, he loves more than you could ever know."

it makes me smile to think of how you look at me. the undeclared adoration in them is too beautiful for words for they could never do it justice.

this is a love letter.
this is a love letter to the one whom i love the most. i doubt you'll ever read but in the things you do i can tell that you'll love me either way.

i love you and i could never fathom a time when i won't. your breath against my skin, hands holding mine.

there is no version of this universe where we aren't meant to be. our souls are two parts of one whole, one flame burning on two candles.

There was a land of sun and flowers,
of sugarcane and ungodly hours.

From summer days the old vines sing
and from aged ones the new vines sing.

Stars burn up the periphery,
Blinding visuals,
laying claims on frozen stakes.

None so bold collapse the all too brave,
Live in fear grow old loving darkness.

Broiling lungs toss beating hearts hearts into glove boxes
hijacked prisoners locked in trunks.

Barrels of wine beat livers bloody blue
Say words in double-entendres
Soaked in beer made dull with water

turns cold to ice blown white
Craters devour souls
blistered snow

Angels form childhood impermanence.
Dead things folded amongst dirt
worms bitter with deceit

fueling rage instructs hate turning clovers into
weeds roll over bodies buried deep
invite them home.